Robert Emmett Owen

(1878–1957)

The Spirit of New England

Robert Emmett Owen

(1878–1957)

The Spirit of New England

Lisa N. Peters

Spanierman Gallery, LLC

45 East 58th Street   New York, NY 10022   Telephone (212) 832-0208   Fax (212) 832-8114   http://www.spanierman.com

LISA N. PETERS, director of research at Spanierman Gallery, New York, and coauthor of the forthcoming catalogue raisonné of the work of John Henry Twachtman (with Ira Spanierman), received her undergraduate degree from Colorado College and her doctorate in art history from the Graduate School of the City University of New York. Her publications include *American Impressionist Masterpieces* (Hugh Lauter Levin, 1991), an essay in *John Twachtman: Connecticut Landscapes,* exhibition catalogue (National Gallery of Art, Washington, D.C., 1989), *James McNeill Whistler* (Smithmark, 1996), *A Personal Gathering: Paintings and Sculpture from the Collection of William I. Koch,* exhibition catalogue (Wichita Art Museum, 1996), *John Twachtman (1853–1902) and the American Scene in the Late Nineteenth Century: The Frontier within the Terrain of the Familiar,* Ph.D. dissertation, City University of New York (University Microfilms, 1996), and *Visions of Home: American Impressionist Images of Suburban Leisure and Country Comfort,* exhibition catalogue (Carlisle, Pa.: Dickinson College, 1997).

Published in the United States of America in 1998 by
Spanierman Gallery, LLC, 45 East 58th Street, New York, NY 10022.

Copyright © 1998 Spanierman Gallery, LLC.

ISBN 0-945936-17-6

Photography: figs. 1–7 Lee Ewing; cats. 1–45 Roz Akin

Editor: Nancy Preu

Design: Marcus Ratliff
Composition: Amy Pyle
Imaging: Center Page
Lithography: Meridian Printing

Contents

Robert Emmett Owen (1878–1957)

The Spirit of New England

ROBERT EMMETT OWEN was raised in extremely humble circumstances. Born in the northwestern Massachusetts town of North Adams, he was brought up by his mother (whose own mother was a native American from a tribe in Curtisville, near Stockbridge, Massachusetts). He never knew his father (pharmacist Robert Willard Owen), who left his mother before he was born. By working as a seamstress, Owen's mother "supported a tiny home for us and saw to it that I had an education," as the artist recalled.[1] During his early school years, Owen began to explore art, creating pencil drawings and watercolors. His skill was recognized by his drawing teacher, Arthur Scribner, who gave his mother a watercolor set, saying: "This is for Robert, he is going to be an artist."[2] In 1895, Owen attended high school at the Drury Academy in his hometown. He excelled in his studies, but when the financial burden became too great for his mother, he left school to work as a clerk and newspaper delivery boy in a local stationery store. Since the store sold art supplies and art magazines, Owen was able to develop friendships with local art teachers and students as well as to have access to drawing materials. In 1897, one of the store's patrons sent some of his drawings to *Life Magazine*. These were accepted and published, launching him in his career as an illustrator.

In the next year, Owen received a scholarship to the newly established Eric Pape School of Art in Boston. During his two years at the school, he took classes in life drawing and composition. To support himself, he held positions at the school as secretary and class monitor and worked at the *Boston Globe* creating comic strips and pen-and-ink drawings that were reproduced as engravings; many of these depicted the Boer War (the war over South African independence from Britain that took place from 1899 to 1902). He also contributed drawings to the *Brown Book of Boston* and *National Magazine*.

Fig. 1. Photograph of Robert Emmett Owen, ca. 1920s, Robert Emmett Owen Papers, Archives of American Art, Smithsonian Institution, Washington, D.C.

Fig. 2. Robert Emmett Owen, pen-and-ink drawing, illustration from *Sketches of Fort Ticonderoga and Vicinity* (Baltimore, Md.: Williams & Wilkins, 1923), p. 9.

Fig. 3. Robert Emmett Owen, *Village Scene*, pen-and-ink drawing, Owen Papers.

In 1900, Owen exhibited at the Boston Art Club, showing a black and white image of a Berkshire home.

Armed with sample illustrations, Owen moved that year to New York City. The first magazine he approached was *Pearson's*, which commissioned him to illustrate two stories written by the actress Clara Morris. In the ten years that followed, Owen created illustrations for the most prominent and popular magazines of his era, including *Frank Leslie's Popular Monthly*, *Delineator*, *Designer*, *Scribner's*, *Harper's Bazaar*, *Century*, *Everybody's*, *Cosmopolitan*, *Success*, *Life*, and *Women's Home Companion*. Owen's skills as an illustrator were wide-ranging. Working primarily in pen and ink, he depicted figures in a proficient manner, conveying clear narratives. He portrayed architectural structures with precision, noting details such as intricate stonework patterns on houses and the crisp lines of Federal-style churches (figs. 2–3). His forté as an illustrator,

however, was landscape imagery, in which he used lines and shading effectively to capture varied textures and effects of light and shadow in nature (fig. 4). In many works, he featured roads as perspectival devices (fig. 5), creating focal points that pull the viewer directly into his scenes.

For ten years, while he was employed as an illustrator, Owen held in abeyance his desire to focus on landscape painting, but in 1910, he had acquired enough income to indulge his primary passion. He recalled that in that year: "I had grown so tired of the tiring grind of the drawing board that upon taking a trip through Connecticut in the blaze of Autumn color, I decided to begin my long-delayed landscape painting career."[3] It was while driving in the countryside near Stamford, Connecticut, that Owen saw a small vacant house on Den Road in Bagnall. He rented it immediately, and along with his wife Miriam (née Rogg), whom he had married in 1903, he settled into life in the

LEFT TO RIGHT:

Fig. 4. Robert Emmett Owen, pen-and-ink, illustration from "Sketches of Fort Ticonderoga," *Harper's Bazaar* 148 (April 1924), p. 639.

Fig. 5. Robert Emmett Owen, *Snow-Covered Road*, pen-and-ink drawing, Owen Papers.

countryside. With nature at his back door, he devoted himself to painting outdoors in all seasons of the year.

Owen was readily accepted by the community of artists working in southern Connecticut. Among his neighbors was sculptor Gutzom Borglum (1867–1941), who frequently invited Owen to paint on his estate in Stamford. One day when Owen was working there, Borglum excitedly reported that he had just received a commission for a national memorial on Mount Rushmore in South Dakota. Borglum invited Owen to see the first model that he created in clay for that project. Another artist with whom Owen associated in Connecticut was Frederick Mulhaupt (1871–1938), a painter of landscapes, marines, and figure subjects rendered in America and Europe. Mulhaupt and Owen frequently went on painting trips together and encouraged each other to explore methods of plein-air painting.

At some point, probably shortly after settling in Connecticut, Owen is known to have studied with Leonard Ochtman (1854–1934), a Dutch-born painter of contemplative and lyrical landscapes that exemplified the American Tonalist style.[4] Owen probably attended the summer classes that Ochtman taught at Grayledge, his home in Mianus (now part of Cos Cob) on the west bank of the Mianus River. In 1912, Ochtman helped to found the Greenwich Society of Artists, and he may have invited Owen to participate in that group's first exhibition, which was held that fall.[5] In the next year, Owen became an official member of the organization; he remained a participant in the Society until 1919. During his years in Connecticut, Owen also exhibited at the Connecticut Academy of Fine Arts in Hartford, to which he was elected a member. In addition, he was included in annuals at New York's National Academy of Design in 1912 and 1913.

In 1919, Owen was invited by J. Temple Gwathmey, president of the Cotton Exchange, to paint at his Virginia estate. There Owen completed twenty images of the Blue Ridge mountains, including one that was twenty feet long. When his host bought all of the works, Owen had the financial means to return to New York, where he resumed his illustration career. In the years that followed, he continued to work for popular magazines as well as to illustrate many children's books, including *Grimm's Fairy Tales* (Cupples and Leon, 1922), Ethel Cook Elliot's *The Little Black Coal* (Frederick A. Stokes Company, 1923), Mabel Powers's *Around an Iroquois Story Fire* (Vehsennonwehs, 1923), Hellen Fuller Orton's *Bobby of Cloverfield Farm* (Stokes, 1922), *Summer at Cloverfield* (Stokes,

1924), and *Mystery of the Little Red School House* (Stokes, 1941). One of his important projects was the creation in 1921 of a group of pen-and-ink drawings of the Crown Point Forts on Lake Champlain that he sold to the *New York Tribune*. The paper published all of his images on one page under the heading "Outpost of Freedom." Two years later, Owen was invited by Stephen Pell to produce pen-and-ink sketches of Fort Ticonderoga, also on Lake Champlain, which Pell was having restored. Owen created over two hundred drawings, some of which were published by *Harper's Bazaar* in 1924, while others were reproduced by Pell in a special edition book (fig. 6).

The year 1923 was significant for Owen. While completing his work for Pell, he conceived of the unique idea of opening his own gallery, in which he would exclusively show and sell his own paintings. Many American artists had been active self-promoters, including Frederic Church, who held gala openings at which his grand-scale canvases were displayed by gaslight, but the actual operation of a gallery devoted to a single artist and run by that artist was unprecedented. Owen began his venture with a small space at 202 Madison Avenue at Thirty-fifth Street, which he announced with a letter to potential patrons that read: "Following my ten years of painting in the hills and woods of New England, I have opened [this gallery] for the presentation to the public of my landscape paintings." The gallery was so well received that he moved about a year later to the Rembrandt Building, next to Carnegie Hall on Fifty-seventh Street, calling his operation, "R. Emmett Owen: New England Landscapes." By 1935, he had moved the gallery again, this time to 20 West Fifty-eighth Street, opposite the Plaza Hotel. His final move was to 681 Madison Avenue, between Sixty-first and Sixty-second streets.

Owen's galleries were quite successful, and according to all accounts, he was very gracious to his patrons, taking the time to share his love of the New England landscape and to discuss his paintings with them. Owen recalled:

Fig. 6. "Entrance to the Place d'Armes or Courtyard of the Fort, pen-and-ink illustration from Fort Ticonderoga," from *Sketches of Fort Ticonderoga and Vicinity* (Baltimore, Md.: Williams & Wilkins, 1923), p. 11.

People usually came to my gallery saying, we saw your New England pictures—so we came in to look or they asked, "did you paint all these?" When assured that I did and that I painted New England subjects because it was my birthplace and because I found old red barns and farmhouses and covered bridges and stone fences were my favorite subjects— and those that had a personal appeal to me. Sometimes I explained that I had started my one-man gallery as an experiment—not knowing how it would be received and had found the majority of those who came had that same interest that I had—particularly business men many of whom were native New Englanders or had grown to like New England from having traveled through it.[6]

As one patron recalled, Owen always extended "the same welcome…to visitors—the same patience in showing the pictures whether the caller was 'in the market' for pictures or not."[7] Among Owen's clients were prosperous figures, leaders of industry and banking as well as artists and educators, including general counsel for General Motors John Thomas Smith; lawyer Paul D. Cravath; Connecticut Senator Raymond Baldwin; Mrs. William Rockefeller; Percy Rockefeller; symphony orchestra conductor Dr. Frank Black; and Secretary of State Edward Stettinius. Many of these collectors were drawn to Owen's works because they had grown up in New England and sought a connection with the quiet and peaceful towns and countrysides that they had enjoyed as youths.

During the 1920s and 1930s, Owen took numerous painting trips around New England. He painted in the Berkshires, and throughout the 1930s, he visited the White Mountain region in central New Hampshire, working in Plymouth, West Plymouth, West Campton, Woodstock, and Twin Mountain. Among his sites were Branford Notch, Lake Winnipesaukee, Mount Washington, Mount Monadnock, and Franconia Notch.

Significant exhibitions of Owen's art were held during the 1930s. Solo shows of his work were held in 1931 at the Public Library of Greenwich, in 1935 at the Hood Museum at Dartmouth College in Hanover, New Hampshire, and in 1936 at Dwight Art Memorial at Mount Holyoke College in Northampton, Massachusetts.

Owen managed to keep his gallery running through the Great Depression, but in 1941, when America entered World War II, he closed it and moved to the New York City suburb of New Rochelle, New York. There he established a studio at the Thomas Paine Memorial Museum. In 1950, two shows of his work were held, at the Albany Institute of History and Art and at the Barbizon Plaza Hotel in New York. In New Rochelle, Owen's energy did not wane. Right until his death in 1957, he was sending out invitations to the public to visit his studio and see his new work.

After settling in New York in 1900, Owen became influenced by the art of prominent American Impressionists, which he viewed in Manhattan galleries. Studying landscapes by artists such as Childe Hassam, Willard Metcalf, John Henry Twachtman, and Theodore Robinson inspired him to paint with vigorous, broken strokes and to utilize a palette of wide-ranging vivid tonalities. Working mostly in the open air and occasionally in the studio from outdoor sketches, he transcribed his subjects in a spontaneous fashion, portraying his forms with loose, irregular strokes in order to convey shifting effects of sunshine and shadow. His aim was to capture his direct visual responses, while also conveying the moods that his sites evoked. By contrast with his drawings, in which he used line to describe form, in his paintings, he suggested form through his brushwork.

Owen found an ideal subject for his paintings in New England. He felt that the landscape of this region afforded an inexhaustible variety of subjects and effects, and he set out to explore the full gamut of its offerings by painting its varied scenery in all seasons of the year. His ability to achieve his goal was noted by William McCormack, who wrote in the *New American*: "The physiology of that country is presented in its varying forms and under the aspects of the changing seasons. [Owen] sets down the facts of nature with a knowing precision and he envelops them with that tender atmosphere which is New England's changeless note."[8] Of the seasons, autumn appears to have been his favorite, and his many views of this subject are resplendent with warm blends of golden yellow, apricot, peach, rust-brown, and red-orange. Owen's images of fall foliage invoke the legacy of the autumnal views by Hudson River School painter Jasper Cropsey. However, instead of the sublime awe that Cropsey expressed, Owen concentrated on the sensuous reality of crackling leaves and hillsides bursting with rich color. In his late career, Owen often focused on winter scenes. Like Twachtman, he realized that snow was rarely white, and he captured its variegated surfaces by blending white impasto with a range of soft colors.

Of the American Impressionists who painted New England, Owen was among the most dedicated to the subject and to capturing its essence before the sweep of modern progress transformed the region. Indeed, he purposefully chose subjects that evoked

New England's past and that suggested its identity as a place where life remained peaceful, simple, and quiet. In a number of paintings, he sought out the old churches dating from the Colonial era that symbolized the Anglo-Saxon New England tradition. In these works (cats. 9–12), he accentuated the crisp geometry of pristine white buildings with their green-shuttered windows, sloping gabled roofs, bell towers, and tapering spires by placing them prominently in his compositions and showing them enframed by natural forms. Choosing canvas formats that echoed the shapes of these structures, he accentuated the symmetrical proportions of the buildings. Like the similar images of colonial churches by Childe Hassam, Owen's views of New England churches echo the search for archetypal American forms that was pursued by architects and designers associated with the Colonial Revival at the turn of the century.

Owen's fascination with typically American subjects is also demonstrated in his images of New England's old farmhouses and barns. In the early twentieth century, such structures were the subject of a significant amount of attention in popular American magazines, where they were praised for having a classical quality of permanence and stability desirable in a time of rapid change. Set behind stone fences and embowered by trees, the dwellings in Owen's paintings evoke the simple pleasures of domestic life in the countryside (cats. 1–8).

Owen's commitment to recording a disappearing America is demonstrated especially in his images of New England's old covered bridges (fig. 7; cats. 13–16). During a time when he was occupied with this subject, he wrote of his fascination with these structures and his unsuccessful quest for funds to complete a series of paintings recording them for posterity:

> For several years past I have given much time to searching out and painting covered bridges throughout New England and while many of these have been washed away by floods and been torn down and replaced by more modern structures I have been able to collect a valuable amount of material in studies and other data of these historic bridges.
>
> Since these are distinctly Early American I have long hoped to paint a really important group of canvases of these beautiful bridges—but thus far insufficient funds have prevented.... I have learned that there are over three hundred of these bridges still in existence although they are rapidly disappearing.[9]

Owen, who used a covered bridge image for his letterhead, hoped to accompany his paintings with descriptions of the "bridges, including their location, date of construction, length etc.," and to exhibit the works and lecture on them throughout the United States.[10]

Indeed, covered bridges summed up the ideals of a lost time in American life. Built by hand from large, slow-growth timbers that were once the pride of New England forests, they were reminders of the unsullied grandeur of the nation's landscape before the rise of the modern timber industry. In his images, Owen featured covered bridges prominently, giving these humble forms a certain monumentality. Detailing their unique shapes, portals, and trusses, he paid tribute to the artistry that went into their creation. He also recorded the way that they harmonized with their settings by capturing the patterned effect of reflections and shadows cast on them from their surroundings.

In other paintings, Owen depicted typical New England landscapes. Instead of broad vistas, he favored intimate perspectives that invite the viewer to enjoy the scene near at hand, and he often focused on a particular aspect of nature. In many of his works, the different trees of New England are his primary subject. Recognizing the individuality of trees, Owen felt they were not motifs to be relegated to the background of a scene, and he often established vantage points looking directly into the midst of a thick glade (cats. 29–30). In these images our attention is drawn to the rhythmic intervals between dark trunks, and to the way that light filters through rustling leaves. In a number of works, Owen gave a particular tree the dominant position (cat. 32), asking us to notice its overall outline and the way that other trees around it played supporting roles, echoing its shape or softening its lines to integrate it into the landscape as a whole. In one series of images, Owen focused on cherry trees (cats. 33–34), capturing the delicacy of cherry blossoms with flickering dabs of pale pink and blue. Reflecting the influence of Japanese prints, the leaves in these works seem to float on the surface of the image, filtering our view of the landscape beyond.

Owen also delighted in studying water. Evoking the art of John Twachtman in his images of brooks, waterfalls, and pools, he varied the rhythm of his brush to accord with the changing flow of moving water and patterns of reflected light on its surface. His ability to adapt his style to the particular qualities of a scene is demonstrated in these works. For example, in *Winter River Scene* (cat. 27), Owen depicted an icebound river in the defining light of late afternoon, capturing the strong contrast between light-struck icy patches edging the waterway and the darkened surface of the river. Taking a low vantage point, Owen provides us with a broad view of the river extending toward the distance. His approach accentuates the scene's stillness, imbuing it with a solemn grandeur. By contrast, in *River Rocks* (cat. 23), Owen took an overhead vantage point looking directly into a pool of water. Here the edges of the pool are not visible and our focus is on the diffused patterns of reflected light and shadow. Painting with typical Impressionist brushwork, Owen used quick dabs of yellow, blue, green, and rust to convey the animated effects of the atmosphere and sunlight and to express nature's flux.

In a number of works, Owen concentrated his attention on New England skies (cats. 36–40). By lowering his horizons, he filled these canvases with the broken and moving shapes of cloud formations. In each, the clusters of clouds convey a different mood. In *Autumn Fields* (cat. 27), Owen evoked the work of Barbizon painter Charles Daubigny. Here, gathering white-gray cloud masses have obscured the sunlight, casting the earth in dark green shadows and conveying a feeling of moodiness and mystery. By contrast, in *Big Clouds, Spring* (cat. 36), while the clouds are again full and thick masses, they are infiltrated by sparkling sunlight, which casts dappled patterns on the earth. The feeling in this painting is more light-hearted and carefree.

Another of Owen's favorite motifs was a curving road that extends directly from the foreground of his canvas (cats. 17–21). The presence of these rutted old back roads gives his works a human perspective, providing the viewer with a vantage point to observe nature and the varied effects of sunlight. Rather than showing roads as routes to travel through the landscape, Owen depicted them as places from which to enjoy the beauty of immediate surroundings. In Owen's images, the meandering roads that follow the undulating grade of the land enhance the appeal of existing nature, suggesting the beneficial imprint of man on the New England landscape. This vision, of course, reflected an ideal that was already being eroded in the early twentieth century by the growth of cities and the spreading network of highways that crossed the region.

Even in his images of mountains or of wilderness scenery in general, Owen rarely portrayed countrysides filled with sublime or spectacular scenery (cats. 41–45). Although his subjects included Mount Washington, Franconia Notch, and other noted peaks in New Hampshire's White Mountains, he generally avoided the depiction of steeply ascending rises seen from great distances, preferring to portray his views from the foothills and to focus on gradual inclines leading to rounded ridges. The gently rising and falling silhouettes of mountain crests echo the rhythmic qualities of trees and brooks below, accentuating harmonious interrelationships in nature.

Owen was not alone in painting Impressionist views of New England, but his works stand out for their ability to encapsulate the spirit of the region in not only its physical attributes but also its essence. As one writer stated: "In some of his larger scenes can be read the rugged strength and determination that has moulded the character of New Englanders."[11] Referred to as "portraits of nature," his paintings were praised for their reality and believability.[12] A critic wrote, "His waters move, his color effects are not merely colors, they are accurate delineations, his trees live, his rocks are component parts of the cosmic scheme of things."[13] Indeed, in his straightforward, unsentimentalized images, Owen celebrated New England's charming, intimate, and familiar qualities. It was just such qualities that endeared the region to a nation in the throes of change. As one writer stated, Owen portrayed "the more picturesque aspects of our country just about the way we like to see it," while another praised him for depicting "our New England countryside in its most attractive aspects."[14] Yet another critic voiced the opinion that due to the human scale of his scenes, Owen's works were "perhaps more suitable for homes than museums."[15] Indeed, the world of pleasant byways marked by old wooden bridges, quaint farmhouses, open, cloud-filled skies, and trickling brooks that Owen conjured is one that we still idealize and desire today.

1. Robert Emmett Owen Papers, autobiographical recollection, Archives of American Art, Smithsonian Institution, Washington, D.C.

2. Owen, autobiographical recollection, Archives of American Art.

3. Owen, autobiographical recollection, Archives of American Art.

4. On Ochtman, see Susan G. Larkin, *The Ochtmans of Cos Cob*, exh. cat. (Greenwich, Conn.: The Bruce Museum, 1989).

5. On the Greenwich Society of Artists, see Susan G. Larkin, "A Regular Rendezvous for Impressionists": The Cos Cob Art Colony, 1882–1920, Ph.D. dissertation, The City University of New York, 1996 (Ann Arbor, Mich.: University of Michigan, 1996), pp. 83–106.

6. Owen, autobiographical recollection, Archives of American Art.

7. Unsourced typescript, Robert Emmett Owen Papers, Archives of American Art.

8. William McCormack, *New American*, quoted in *Robert Emmett Owen, 1878–1957*, exh. cat. (Boston: Vose Galleries of Boston, 1980), p. 7.

9. Owen, autobiographical recollection, Archives of American Art.

10. Owen, autobiographical recollection, Archives of American Art.

11. "R. Emmett Owen's Gift to the World," *National Business Review*, July 1926, p. 44.

12. "R. Emmett Owen's Gift to the World," p. 44.

13. Unsourced article from a Greenwich, Connecticut, newspaper, Robert Emmett Owen Papers, Archives of American Art.

14. Unsourced article from a Greenwich, Connecticut, newspaper, "Announcement for Exhibit (Greenwich Public Library)," March 9, 1939. Robert Emmett Owen Papers, Archives of American Art.

15. Untitled article in *New Hampshire Troubadour* (January 1935). Robert Emmett Owen Papers, Archives of American Art.

1.

Old New Hampshire Lake House, ca. 1920s–1930s

Oil on canvas laid down on board

12 × 16 in. (30.5 × 40.6 cm)

In 1884, the critic Mariana van Rensselaer praised "those old farm-houses built by Dutch or English settlers, which still survive in many a quiet spot" as distinctly American, stating that "nothing could be more simple, more utilitarian, more without thought of architectural effectiveness."[1] Such adulation for old colonial homes continued to be voiced into the early twentieth century. In a rapidly changing modern world, the simple dwellings represented the preservation of traditional American values, and their clean lines and emphatic horizontals were perceived as reflecting a quality of permanence and stability that was desirable in the era of the skyscraper and the motor car.

Echoing written tributes, many artists were inspired by the the nostalgia that colonial dwellings evoked, and Impressionists, including Childe Hassam and Willard Metcalf, were among the most devoted to seeking out old homes and recording them on canvas.

With his passion for depicting the places in New England that recalled an earlier time, Owen was naturally drawn to this motif as well, and spent time finding old farmhouses that remained intact. His approach is demonstrated in *Old New Hampshire Lake House*, in which he featured a typical wooden dwelling with a gabled doorway. On the front lawn, a sweep extends into an old well, revealing the self-sufficiency of the homeowners. Owen echoed the horizontal lines of the structure in his choice of canvas format, imbuing the work with the serenity evoked by its subject matter.

1. M[ariana] G. van Rensselaer, "American Country Dwellings, pt. 1," *Century Magazine* 32 (May 1886): 3–4.

2.

The Gay House, near New London, New Hampshire, ca. 1920s–1930s

Oil on canvasboard

12 × 16 in. (30.5 × 40.6 cm)

Inscribed on verso: *Built in 1790–1797 / Old Homestead and Antique Shop / Near New London N.H / The Gay House*

Like the American Impressionist Willard Metcalf, Owen enjoyed depicting the old American homes of New England that had historic importance. This interest is revealed in his view of the Gay House, located in the southwest New Hampshire town of New London. As the artist carefully noted, this dwelling was built in the last decade of the eighteenth century and housed an antique shop at the time he painted the canvas.

Owen depicted the scene in the early winter. Only one tree still bears yellow-brown autumnal foliage, while others are bare, allowing the architectural forms set in from the roadway to be easily distinguished. The gray and rust-brown buildings, which enclose a courtyard, complement the earth tones in the landscape, suggesting the way that the house and its outbuildings had become harmonized with their setting over time.

3.

Winter Twilight, ca. 1910s–1930s

Oil on canvas

35¼ × 44¼ in. (89.5 × 112.4 cm)

Signed lower right: *R. Emmett Owen*

In *Winter Twilight,* Owen studied the effect of a landscape enveloped in the subdued illumination of dusk. In the sky, the sun is diffused through a thick cloud cover, while across the landscape, long lavender shadows are cast by buildings and trees. With the pink glow of sunset reflected in their walls, a house and barn set behind a stone fence evoke the comforts to be found within. Indeed, this painting was perhaps similar to Owen's *New England House, Winter,* which a critic felt exemplified Owen's "skill in the treatment of light," remarking in 1936: "Here the coolness of the snow is emphasized by warm tones of the house and barn."[1]

1. "New England Scenes by Robert E. Owen," *Springfield Sun, Union & Republic,* January 19, 1936.

4.

Cabin in the Woods, ca. 1910s–1930s

Oil on canvas
10 × 14 in. (25.4 × 35.6 cm)
Signed lower right: *R. Emmett Owen*
Signed on verso: *R. Emmett Owen*

To capture the essence of New England, Owen sought his subjects both in settled rural areas and in the region's back country. He chose the latter subject for *Cabin in the Woods*. Here he portrayed a wooden building, possibly serving as a saw mill, surrounded by tall trees that are filled with the brilliant golden tones of autumnal leaves. Although the site appears to be deep in the woods, the presence of two horses pulling a wagon indicate the presence of a nearby community.

5.

Study of John Burroughs House, West Park, New York, ca. 1910s

Oil on canvas

25¼ × 30¼ in. (64.1 × 76.8 cm)

Signed lower right: *R. Emmett Owen*

Inscribed on verso: *Slabsides / Study of John Burroughs / Winter Parkway /*
   Home of John Burroughs at West Park NY

In 1895, the naturalist writer John Burroughs (1837–1921) sought a retreat where he could write and study nature directly. Traveling a mile and a half from his home in West Park on the Hudson River, ten miles south of Kingston, he found his ideal site in the midst of the woods. There he built a rustic cabin that he named Slabsides. During retreats to this residence until his death in 1921, he wrote some of his best-known essays and entertained important figures including Theodore Roosevelt, John Muir, Thomas Edison, and Henry Ford.

Owen, who shared Burroughs's love of the repose offered by nature, may have been among those to make a pilgrimage to Slabsides, and his decision to depict the house suggests his appreciation for the writer. Portraying new leaves gracing the bare trees that surround the small dwelling and bringing out the lavender and mauve tonalities of the bark walls of the home, Owen captured the picturesqueness of Slabsides in a landscape in which the first burst of spring has begun to come forth. For Burroughs, Slabsides provided a fresh perspective. He wrote:

> A slab is the first cut from the loaf, which we call the crust, and which the children reject, but which we older ones often prefer. I wanted to take a fresh cut of life,—something that had the bark on, or, if you please, that was like a well-browned and hardened crust. After three years I am satisfied with the experiment. Life has a different flavor here.[1]

For Owen, who had also retreated to the country when he moved to Bagnall, Connecticut, in 1910, such words may have had personal resonance.

1. John Burroughs, "Wild Life about My Cabin," from *Far and Near* (Boston: Houghton Mifflin, 1904), p. 133.

6.

Red Barn, ca. 1910s–1920s

Oil on canvas
16 × 20 in. (40.6 × 50.8 cm)
Signed lower right: *R. Emmett Owen*

Owen's delight in depicting the motifs that characterized New England is demonstrated in *Red Barn.* Here his subject is the type of shingled, weathered rust-red structure that can be found throughout the rural countrysides of Connecticut, Vermont, and New Hampshire. However, showing the barn broadly filling the canvas, Owen asks the viewer to contemplate it on its own terms rather than seeing it merely as part of the passing scenery. From our direct angle, the thickly painted walls and the adjoined buildings imbue the humble subject with a sculpturesque monumentality that suggests the enduring value of this icon of New England life.

7.

Autumn Harvest, ca. 1910s–1930s

Oil on canvas

25 × 30 in. (63.3 × 76.2 cm)

Signed lower right: *R. Emmett Owen*

In this painting, Owen celebrated the sense of peace and abundance evoked
by the autumn harvest in a rural countryside. Our view is through a field of
haystacks to several small farm buildings set within a cluster of trees. On the
orange-peach toned hills, other farmhouses may be seen. The countryside is
settled, but its broad areas of open land suggest a feeling of freedom and pos-
sibility. The golden light that suffuses the scene fills it with a sense of warmth
and contentment.

8.

Rural Village, ca. 1910s–1920s

Oil on canvas
18 × 20 in. (45.7 × 50.8 cm)
Signed lower right: *R. Emmett Owen*

In *Rural Village*, Owen used a painterly approach to depict a verdant countryside where the homes of a peaceful village are scattered at wide intervals.
Instead of detailing architectural or natural forms, he conveyed the way that
they flowed together harmoniously. The painting captures a characteristic of
many New England towns, especially in New Hampshire and Vermont, where
communities were not tightly knit villages, but clusters of homes set at wide
intervals across rolling landscapes. The low vantage point in the work makes
us aware of the broad expanses of green meadows and open hillsides that typify
the New England landscape.

9.

Country Church, ca. 1910s–1930s

Oil on canvas
26 × 34 in. (66 × 86.4 cm)
Signed lower right: *R. Emmett Owen*

In the early twentieth century, the colonial churches of New England were a favorite subject for American Impressionist Childe Hassam, who celebrated America's past in his images of these simple, functional buildings with their crisp white walls and attenuated spires. Like Hassam, and a number of other American Impressionist painters, Owen found beauty in the humble houses of worship that were picturesquely situated in New England's rural country-side. His approach is demonstrated in this painting. Here our view is toward the side and roof of a typical country church. Above the building's belfry, its spire appears to rise into the clouds, suggesting the church's role as a link between terrestrial and celestial realms. In the facade of the white building, Owen recorded multi-hued reflections and shadows that serve to connect the building integrally with the sunlit landscape. With this sparkling image, Owen, like Hassam, creates a paean to the New England of an earlier time.

10.

Church with Spired Steeple, ca. 1910s–1930s

Oil on canvas
34¼ × 44 in. (87 × 111.8 cm)
Signed lower right: *R. Emmett Owen*

In this autumnal scene, our gaze is drawn up a hillside covered with brown- and gold-toned grasses to a simple white church with a square tower and green-shuttered windows that is offset against a line of rust-beige trees. A tall already-bare tree at the center of the composition echoes the thrust of the tower, as if to convey the harmonious link between man and nature in this quiet place. Indeed, Owen suggests that the peaceful spiritual experience of the inner chapel is continued in the outdoors, where dry leaves gently rustle and the sparkling variety of turning fall foliage is fully emergent. By contrast with the church, however, the old wooden lean-to beside it reminds us of the more commonplace aspects of New England life.

11.

Greenfield Hill Church, Connecticut, ca. 1910s

Oil on canvas
20 × 16 in. (50.8 × 40.6 cm)
Signed lower left: *R. Emmett Owen*
Titled on verso: *Greenfield Hill Church*

Situated in the northern part of Fairfield, Connecticut, Greenfield Hill was incorporated in 1725. The gem of this colonial town is the Congregational Church, which faces the village green and is framed by the longstanding plantings that link all the old buildings at this town's center. It is this historic structure that Owen portrayed in *Greenfield Hill Church, Connecticut.* Taking his view from a somewhat elevated vantage point, Owen included the church's front facade, with its Palladian-style window directly above its entryway, its open belfry, and its tall, pointed spire. Showing the white church illuminated by a bright midday sunlight, Owen captured its crisp geometry and graceful symmetry, revealing the qualities that have long made this structure the pride of its region.

12.

New Hampshire Street with Church, ca. 1920s–1930s

Oil on canvas

18 × 20 in. (45.7 × 50.8 cm)

Signed lower left: *R. Emmett Owen*

In *New Hampshire Street with Church*, Owen depicted a view through the main street of a small New Hampshire town. At our near left is a colonial church with a columned facade, while old homes face each other on either side of the thoroughfare. Here Owen juxtaposed the typical Impressionist tones of lavender and pale green, but instead of broken Impressionist dabs, his brushwork is more forceful, consisting of firm, sustained strokes. With this method, he emphasized the lines of bare trees, their branches extending across the road, and the outlines of buildings. Moving away from a concern with effects of light to concentrate on the patterns on the work's surface, in *New Hampshire Street with Church*, Owen adopted a Post-Impressionist approach.

13.

Smith Bridge, Plymouth, New Hampshire, ca. 1920s–1930s

Oil on canvas

25 × 30 in. (63.5 × 76.2 cm)

Signed lower right: *R. Emmett Owen*

Inscribed on verso: *New Hampshire Covered Bridge, W. Plymouth N.H.*

For Owen, the covered bridges of New England were a source of fascination, and he hoped at one time to create a full survey of "these distinctly early American" structures "before they were washed away by floods or torn down or replaced by modern structures."[1] Although he painted many views of covered bridges, due to a lack of funds, he was never able to complete the survey. Depicting a site on the Baker River two-and-one-half miles west of the town of Plymouth, in New Hampshire's White Mountains, this painting portrays the Smith Bridge, which was built in 1850 and destroyed by fire in 1993. In his image, Owen recorded the beauty of this old covered bridge set in a wooded countryside. Capturing the soft reflected colors in the weathered walls of the simple, solidly crafted gabled form, Owen demonstrated the way that the bridge had become harmoniously merged with its surroundings.

1. Robert Emmett Owen Papers, autobiographical recollection, Archives of American Art, Smithsonian Institution, Washington, D.C.

14.

Covered Bridge, ca. 1910s–1930s

Oil on canvas
27 × 36⅛ in. (68.6 × 91.7 cm)
Signed lower right: *R. Emmett Owen*

With their compact forms and straightforward designs, the covered bridges of New England were perfectly in tune with the quiet, intimate countryside in which they were situated. In this painting, Owen conveys the sympathetic relationship between a bridge and its surroundings. The light-toned wood of the structure attracts the day's dappled sunlight, while the cool, darkened interior of the bridge offers a place for a quick refuge. Indeed, showing a glimpse into the bridge, Owen was perhaps alluding to the fact that old covered bridges often served dual purposes, as passageways and as meeting places for long-established village communities.

15.

Covered Bridge at Stevens Falls, Barnet, Vermont, ca. 1910s–1930s

Oil on canvas

12 × 16 in. (30.5 × 40.6 cm)

Signed lower left: *R. Emmett Owen*

Titled on verso: *Covered Bridge and Stephens* [sic] *Falls, Barnet, Vermont*

For this painting, Owen traveled to the town of Barnet in northeastern Vermont. Here his subject is a covered bridge, still existing today, that crosses over Stevens Falls on the Stevens River, a tributary of the Connecticut River. Taking his view from below the bridge, Owen focused on the rapidly moving cascade flowing freely down a rocky river bed. With its ends obscured by trees and its open latticed supports, the wooden bridge seems part of nature, adding to the lively scene rather than distracting from it, as a more modern structure would be likely to do. Owen's skill as an artist is reflected in his sensitivity to this unity between the manmade and the natural.

16.

Stinson Mountain, Columbia Covered Bridge, Rumney, New Hampshire, ca. 1920s–1930s

Oil on canvasboard

12 × 16 in. (30.5 × 40.6 cm)

Signed lower right: *R. Emmett Owen*

Inscribed on verso: *Stinson Mt. / Rumney / Covered Bridge*

In most of the works in his covered bridge series, Owen took close-up viewpoints on his subjects, revealing the tones and textures of old wooden walls. By contrast, in *Stinson Mountain, Columbia Covered Bridge, Rumney, New Hampshire,* Owen's vantage point was from a distance looking toward an old red structure situated in the foothills of Stinson Mountain, which rises 2,870 feet. In the painting, Owen captured the essence of a countryside that was relatively unsettled, but not rugged or wild. Shown with the lavender glow of sunset reflected on its facade, Stinson Mountain shelters the landscape below, while the rust-red bridge is nestled comfortably in a landscape of similarly toned trees.

17.

October, ca. 1910s–1930s

Oil on canvas
40 × 50½ in. (101.6 × 128.3 cm)
Signed lower right: *R. Emmett Owen*

Probably because he loved traveling through the back country of New England, the region's old roads were a favorite subject for Owen. Indeed, one critic referred to him as an "automobile tourist" who ventured "with palette and brush, ready to carry away with him the best there is of New England scenery."[1] A sense of Owen's delight in the typical winding passageways that crossed through the rolling terrain of New England is conveyed in *October.* Here a soft light filters through the trees, some of which reveal the richness of fall foliage and others of which are already bare, casting flickering reflections on the ruddy surface of an unpaved road. While sunlight illuminates a bend in the road that leads us forward, the lavender background suggests the presence of hilly terrain ahead. Applying his strokes vigorously to capture fleeting effects of light and shadow, Owen expressed his direct response to a lively subject.

1. Unsourced article from a Greenwich, Connecticut, newspaper, March 5, 1931, Robert Emmett Owen Papers, Archives of American Art, Smithsonian Institution, Washington, D.C.

18.

Morning, Winter on the Farm Road, Connecticut, ca. 1910s

Oil on canvas

18 × 20 in. (45.7 × 50.8 cm)

Signed lower left: *R. Emmett Owen*

Titled on verso: *Morning Winter on the Farm Road, Conn.*

The roads near Owen's home in Bagnall, Connecticut, where he lived from 1910 to 1920, provided him with inspiration during all seasons of the year. He loved to capture the way that these thoroughfares gave structure to nature, establishing order in densely wooded areas or highlighting the intrinsic flow of a countryside's topography. We can see this interest in *Morning Winter on the Farm Road, Connecticut.* Here rutted tracks in a snow-covered road passing through the countryside provide a human perspective, while Owen delighted in capturing the blue-toned shadows cast from the bare-limbed trees in the snow's white surface. Owen's approach links him with the many other French and American Impressionists who enjoyed recording the tonal qualities of sun and shadow on snow-covered roads.

19.

Late Afternoon, Autumn, ca. 1910s–1930s

Oil on canvas
24¼ × 30 in. (62.2 × 76.2 cm)
Signed lower right: *R. Emmett Owen*

In *Late Afternoon, Autumn,* Owen explored the effect of a hazy atmosphere on a quiet countryside in the peak of the fall season. The painting recalls the legacy of Hudson River School artist Jasper Cropsey's images of the Catskills in autumn in which thin mists enveloped landscapes in soft blends of rust, gold-yellow, and red-orange. However, instead of a dramatic view across a broad expanse—the type of image that was Cropsey's speciality—Owen presents us with a civilized road, lined by stone fences, that curves through a peaceful countryside. The hill before us is a shimmering mass of pale rust and orange, but its rounded contours suggest that this is an accesssible human-scaled land-scape rather than one evoking thoughts of the sublime.

20.

Dirt Road in the Woods, ca. 1910s–1930s

Oil on canvas

16 × 20 in. (40.6 × 50.8 cm)

Signed lower right: *R. Emmett Owen*

In *Dirt Road in the Woods,* Owen captured the quiet feeling of a landscape at the end of winter. Traces of ice remain in the rutted tracks in the road that curves through the landscape, while bare trees are silhouetted against hills seen through the veil of a pale lavender- and peach-toned mist. Complementing the work's soft tonalities, Owen departed from his usually vigorous brush handling to paint with delicate strokes and thin washes of pigment.

21.

Spring, ca. 1944

Oil on canvasboard

12 × 16 inches (30.5 × 40.6 cm)

Signed lower right: *R. Emmett Owen*

Titled, dedicated, and dated on verso: *Spring to Sylvia and Bob /*
Christmas 1944 from Robert

A direct painter who enjoyed depicting nature with as much veracity as possible, Owen was also attuned to the decorative possibilities that his sites presented. Roads with their linear qualities lent themselves, in particular, to consciously composed designs. In *Spring*, Owen used the road image to create an abstract arrangement. Suggestive of the flat patterns in Japanese prints, the sinuous line of the road shown in this work seems flush with the picture plane, while other landscape elements are reduced to tones, lines, and shapes, which Owen grouped to create a lively pattern.

22.

Summer Reflections, ca. 1910s–1930s

Oil on canvas

26¾ × 34¼ in. (67.9 × 87 cm)

Signed lower right: *R. Emmett Owen*

Like other Impressionist painters, Owen took pleasure in portraying reflections and shadows on water. Traveling into the heart of the New England countryside, he sought places that were conducive to exploring this subject. In *Summer Reflections*, he chose to depict a lake surrounded by thick trees, their golden-toned boughs illuminated by hot summer sunlight. With its glimmering reflections and slightly ruffled surface, the cool lake provides a counterforce to the heat of the day. Painted throughout with thick impasto scumbled to produce a rough-textured surface, *Summer Reflections* seems imbued with the heavy, lazy feeling of the season represented.

23.

River Rocks, ca. 1910s–1930s

Oil on canvas
25¼ × 35⅝ in. (64.1 × 90.4 cm)
Signed lower left: *R. Emmett Owen*

In *River Rocks,* Owen chose an overhead view of the rustling surface of a river bed. From this angle, the viewer is made aware of the patterns created by scattered rocks and the glistening tones of reflections in the water. Owen's use of an intimate perspective, an aerial vantage point, abrupt cropping, and broken dabs of color make this one of his most typically Impressionist works.

24.

Brook in Autumn, ca. 1910s–1930s

Oil on canvas

27⅛ × 36 in. (68.9 × 91.4 cm)

Signed lower left: *R. Emmett Owen*

For Owen, the fall season offered endless diversity, and he sought to capture its varied moods. Whereas in many of his scenes, he depicted cloudy, hazy, autumn days evoking pensiveness in the viewer, in *Brook in Autumn*, he captured a feeling of buoyancy and cheerfulness. In this scene, the still-green countryside, with its undulating swells of land, and the gold- and orange-red toned trees are vividly illuminated by warm sunlight. The quiet brook, which flows through the valley, adds to the animated spirit of the image. It was for works such as *Brook in Autumn* that a critic commented as early as 1910 that "Mr. Owen paints New England as one loves to see it, and his hills, lakes, and rivers … are most aptly portrayed."[1]

1. "Owen's Paintings Shown at Library, Greenwich, Connecticut," unsourced newspaper clipping, February 29, 1910, Robert Emmett Owen Papers, Archives of American Art, Smithsonian Institution, Washington, D.C.

25.

Marsh Scene, ca. 1910s–1930s

Oil on canvas

25 × 30¼ in. (63.5 × 76.3 cm)

In this view of an inlet flowing through a quiet marsh, Owen used his brush rhythmically to record nature's varied textures. For windswept leaves, he painted with staccato touches of orange-red, yellow-orange, and tan-gold, whereas for the grassy shores of the inlet, he used vigorously cross-hatched strokes. He recorded the silvery surface of the water with broader, more fluid brushwork. The result is a work that brings this tranquil locale to life. The two empty rowboats in the foreground provide the viewer with an entry point into the work, drawing our attention to the sinuous curve of the waterway through the scene.

26.

The River in January, ca. 1910s–1930s

Oil on canvas
18 × 20 in. (45.7 × 50.8 cm)
Signed lower left: *R. Emmett Owen*

Brooks and rivers bound in snow and ice presented an opportunity for Impressionist painters to study the coloristic effects of reflections and shadows on icy waterways as well as on varied ground textures. Like American Impressionists John Twachtman and Willard Metcalf, Owen explored these facets in *The River in January*. In the slow surface of the river, he noted rippled patterns of lavender and silvery gray over rust-brown depths. The blue shadows in the snow and the pink tone in the atmosphere reveal Owen's full affiliation with the Impressionist viewpoint.

27.

Winter River Scene, ca. 1920s–1930s

Oil on canvas

25 × 40 in. (63.5 × 101.6 cm)

Signed lower right: *R. Emmett Owen*

Winter River Scene is one of Owen's most dramatic paintings. Probably rendered during a trip to New Hampshire, the work presents a view of a dark river emerging from a covering of ice and snow. While sunlight illuminates the scene, creating reflections in the water and accentuating the curved outlines of snow patches, the light is hard and cold, serving to define form rather than to disperse it in the typical Impressionist manner. The result is a work that encapsulates the deep chill of midwinter in the woods of New England. At the same time, with the pattern of the dark water offset by the white snow, *Winter River Scene* reveals Owen's refined decorative sensibility.

28.

Brook Scene, ca. 1910s–1930s

Oil on canvas

36 × 22 in. (91.4 × 55.9 cm)

Signed lower right: *R. Emmett Owen*

For this scene of a waterfall cascading through a narrow gorge, Owen used a vertical composition to focus our attention directly on the falls and on the motion of the water, which is the primary subject of this work. Like John Henry Twachtman, who took a similar approach in his 1890s views of the waterfall on his property in Greenwich, Connecticut, Owen varied the force and thickness of his paints to convey the changing rhythms of the cascade. The work depicts Owen's favorite season, and the autumnal tones in the trees are echoed in the surfaces of the rocks, enlivening the composition.

29.

A Woodland Study, ca. 1910s–1930s

Oil on canvas
21¾ × 15¼ in. (55.2 × 38.7 cm)
Signed lower right: *R. Emmett Owen*

To paint this work, Owen traveled into the midst of a deep woods and set his easel down under a dense covering of yellow-green leaves. His interest was clearly in capturing the quietude of this secluded place. Indeed, without a vista in sight, the viewer is encouraged to focus on the effect of sunlight filtering through the leafage and illuminating the inner world of the forest. While Owen painted the trunks of trees with firm broad strokes, revealing their strength and endurance, he depicted foliage with quick flecks of color, capturing nature's evanescence.

30.

Autumn Woodland, ca. 1910s–1930s

Oil on canvas

25⅛ × 34 in. (63.8 × 86.4 cm)

Signed lower right: *R. Emmett Owen*

As in *A Woodland Study* (cat. 29), in *Autumn Woodland*, Owen depicted a view of a forest interior. However, rather than focusing on transitory properties of light and form, in this work, Owen interpreted his subject in spiritual terms. From the cool, darkened interior of the woods, our gaze is drawn upward to the bower of shimmering gold- and orange-toned leaves overhead. Lit from above by bright sunlight, this glittering ceiling evokes the hallowed clerestory of a religious sanctuary.

31.

Spruces in the Last Snow, ca. 1910s–1930s

Oil on canvas

16 × 20½ in. (40.6 × 51.4 cm)

Signed lower right: *R. Emmett Owen*

Inscribed on verso: *The Last of Winter / Spruces in the Last Snow*

    Near Win[illeg.] *Hill*

In *Spruces in the Last Snow,* Owen captured the heartiness of evergreen trees standing firmly in the forest. While snow on the ground has largely melted, heralding the end of winter, the trees appear not to be significantly affected by the changing season. By accentuating their dark green tones and their strong patterned forms silhouetted against the gray-blue sky, Owen conveys their enduring strength. His vigorous, decisive brushwork perfectly suits his subject matter.

32.

Stone Fence, ca. 1910s–1930s

Oil on canvas

40¼ × 36¼ in. (102.2 × 92 cm)

Signed lower right: *R. Emmett Owen*

Owen enjoyed selecting vantage points for his works that focused the viewer's attention on the motif in a scene that he felt to be most important. In *Stone Fence*, his lowered angle of vision is clearly intended to draw our gaze upward to the firm branches of an evergreen tree, possibly a Norway pine. Shown silhouetted against a sky of broken clouds, the tree has a proud and confident presence. Trees behind it seem equally independent and unbowed by the wind coursing across the hilltop. By capturing the strength of solitary trees, Owen expressed his respect for these natural forms, which many artists render mainly as background elements. At the same time, he may have painted the tree as a metaphor for himself, evoking the isolation of his work and the fortitude with which he carried it out.

33.

Cherry Tree Blossoms, ca. 1910s–1930s

Oil on canvas
20 × 24 inches (50.8 × 61 in.)
Signed lower left: *R. Emmett Owen*

In *Cherry Tree Blossoms*, Owen again isolated a single tree. In this case, his choice was not a sturdy evergreen, but a delicate cherry tree in full flower. To capture the essence of his subject, Owen painted the tree's leaves with tiny dabs of pale pink and white pigment applied with light, short strokes. With this approach, he conveyed the fluttering movement of the blossoms. Rendered in soft tones of lavender, mauve, and light green, the undefined background evokes the soft misty quality of a spring morning, while allowing the pale-toned blossoming tree to stand out prominently in the composition.

34.

Cherry Blossoms, ca. 1910s–1930s

Oil on canvasboard

22 × 18 in. (55.9 × 45.7 cm)

Signed lower left: *R. Emmett Owen*

The cherry tree in bloom was one of Owen's favorite motifs. Here he captured the subject at its most evanescent. Against a misty green atmospheric setting, white-pink blossoms seem to be free-floating, held aloft by wind. The result is a patterned surface that makes this work straddle the line between a realistic and an abstract interpretation of nature.

35.

Across the Valley, ca. 1910s–1930s

Oil on canvas

16 × 20 in. (40.6 × 50.8 cm)

Signed lower right: *R. Emmett Owen*

In *Across the Valley,* Owen laid down thick paint with broad, quick strokes, capturing the overall patterned qualities of a rolling landscape of meadows marked by lines of trees that lead to a range of blue hills. While the trees are rendered in highly generalized terms, it is clearly their presence that gives structure to the scene. Owen captured their varied shapes with lively, gestural strokes that suggest their animated qualities. The scene is one of Owen's most abstract, revealing his interest in capturing nature's vitality through the energy of his brushwork and his attention to coloristic relationships.

36.

Big Clouds, Spring, ca. 1910s–1930s

Oil on canvas

50 × 40 in. (127 × 101.6 cm)

Signed lower left: *R. Emmett Owen*

During his travels across the hills of New England, Owen often found himself most compelled by the beauty of cloud-filled skies. To focus on this subject, he frequently chose a low vantage point, filling three-quarters of a canvas with sky. His approach is demonstrated in *Big Clouds, Spring*. Here, standing near the crest of a hill, he draws our gaze upward to focus on the motion of billowing cumulus clouds. While sunlight has broken through an opening in the clouds, the swirling energy of the white masses is a forewarning of a shift in the weather. The variable light in the work and the vital energy of landscape forms suggest the changeability that is the essence of the spring season. The large size of this canvas, combined with the intimacy of the perspective, draws the viewer directly into the scene.

37.

Autumn Fields, ca. 1910s–1930s

Oil on canvas
30 × 40 in. (76.2 × 101.6 cm)
Signed lower left: *R. Emmett Owen*

In *Autumn Fields,* Owen established a low horizon line, drawing our attention from a rural landscape, cast in shadows, to a brilliantly lit open sky filled with broken clouds. By depicting trees with autumnal leaves set into relief against a cluster of full clouds, Owen accentuated the vivacity of the sky. At the same time, the flickers of light that penetrate the hazy atmosphere create a pensive mood, conveying the essential mystery in nature. Owen's use of tone to evoke mood suggests his appreciation for the art of the French Barbizon School.

38.

New Hampshire Hills, ca. 1920s–1930s

Oil on canvas
25¼ × 29¾ in. (64.1 × 75.6 cm)
Signed lower left: *R. Emmett Owen*

During his ventures into the hills of New Hampshire, Owen frequently portrayed the landscape at dawn and dusk, capturing the range of poetic light effects that such times afforded. His fascination with evening light is revealed in *New Hampshire Hills*. In this image, Owen recorded the dark, dusty lavender and olive-green tone of the shadowed hills and the faded blue tone of the sky. While the long curving lines of the landscape and their subdued tonalities evoke the serenity of approaching evening, the clouds overhead seem to have recently emerged to a position of significance in the landscape. Directly above, fleecy cumulus clouds gather force, while over the hills, bullet-like clouds have begun to spread across the sky. The painting reveals Owen's ability to discern the forces in nature that were most alive and make them emerge for the viewer.

39.

Autumn Clouds, ca. 1910–1920s

Oil on canvasboard
12 × 16 in. (30.5 × 40.6 cm)
Signed lower right: *R. Emmett Owen*
Titled on verso: *Autumn Clouds*

Whereas in *Big Clouds, Spring* (cat. 36), Owen focused on nuances of light and shadow within thick cloud masses, in *Autumn Clouds,* he painted his subject very rapidly and freely with broad brush handling, capturing the energy and tonal properties of his subject through the movement of his strokes and the way that he overlaid tones. As a result, it is the brushwork motion itself that draws our attention first in this work, revealing Owen's ability to take an abstract approach to nature when he felt it to be appropriate.

40.

Breezy Morning, ca. 1910s–1930s

Oil on canvasboard
12 × 16 in. (30.5 × 40.6 cm)
Signed lower right: *R. Emmett Owen*

As in his other images of clouds, in *Breezy Morning,* Owen portrayed a thin strip of landscape to provide a sense of place and scale, while the real subject of his work is the energetic cirrus clouds that form long streamers across the blue sky. Applying long, broad strokes, as well as lively, choppy dabs of white, Owen expressed the unconstrained freedom that was the essence of his subject.

41.

River Road in Autumn, ca. 1920s–1930s

Oil on canvas

23¼ × 30 in. (59 × 76.2 cm)

Signed lower right: *R. Emmett Owen*

In this vivid canvas, Owen focused on the brilliant tonal qualities of fall in the mountains of New England. Possibly depicting a view of the east branch of the Pemigewasset River near Lincoln, New Hampshire, Owen provides us with a vantage point along a curving road that parallels a recently thawed waterway. Drawing our gaze upward, he directs us to the rounded knobs of a wooded mountain range suffused in the brilliant orange-reds of fall foliage at its peak. Only a few dashes of green indicate the presence of evergreens or trees that have yet to turn. The repetition of undulating lines in the mountains and the river reveals the kinds of subtle associations in nature to which Owen was especially attuned.

44.

Franconia Range, Woodstock, New Hampshire, ca. 1920s–1930s

Oil on canvas

25⅛ × 34⅛ in. (64 × 87 cm)

Signed lower right: *R. Emmett Owen*

Titled on label on verso: *Franconia Range, Woodstock, New Hampshire*

The Franconia Range in the White Mountains was a favorite subject for the Hudson River School artists who gathered in the town of North Conway in the early nineteenth century. From this base, artists including Jasper Cropsey and Benjamin Champney portrayed views of dramatic scenery that captured the vast expanses of the open countryside. In his images of the White Mountains, Owen downplayed the sublime features of his subject matter, preferring to appeal to our senses rather than to our sense of awe. His approach is demonstrated in *Franconia Range, Woodstock, New Hampshire.* In this image, Owen depicted New Hampshire's highest peaks with Mount Flume or Mount Liberty on the right, but instead of making the mountains our focus, he showed them as a thin lavender line seen at the horizon. He draws our attention mainly to the vibrant autumnal tones and lively textures of the landscape directly before us. Using thick dabs of pigment applied with brushstrokes that vary in rhythm, Owen captured the rich coloristic properties of a peaceful valley in the fall.

It is possible that this painting was included with the title of *Franconia Range* in Owen's 1936 exhibition at Mount Holyoke College in Northampton, Massachusetts, of which a critic remarked: "One of the most pleasing of the autumn scenes is 'Franconia Range.'" The mountains raise their sharp peaks in the distance behind an expanse of gorgeous autumn coloring."[1]

1. "New England Scenes by Robert E. Owen," *Springfield Sun, Union & Republic* (January 19, 1936).

45.

Clouds over a Lake and Mountains, ca. 1920s–1930s

Oil on canvas

42¼ × 60 in. (107.3 × 152.4 cm)

Signed lower right: *R. Emmett Owen*

In *Clouds over a Lake and Mountains,* Owen's subject is probably Lake Winne-pesaukee in central New Hampshire. By creating a low horizon line, Owen conveyed the scale of this lake, which is one of the largest lakes in New England. Indeed, this is among the artist's most far-reaching views. It is nonetheless not a painting that evokes nature's sublime force. The surface of the lake is smooth and calm, while Owen's signature autumnal trees provide a gentle transition to the water below. The mountains in the distance curve downward at the center of the canvas, echoing the sinuous line of trees in the foreground. In the sky, a hint of sunset is present in the gathering clouds, which cast their glow on the range below, further imbuing the work with quiet unity.

Chronology

1878
born January 30 in North Adams, Massachusetts

1895
began art training at the Drury Academy, North Adams

1897
worked at stationery store in North Adams
pen-and-ink drawings published in *Life Magazine*

1898
moved to Boston, where he attended Eric Pape School of Art on a scholarship; worked in life and costume composition classes; held position of secretary for the school and class monitor
produced comic strips for the *Boston Globe,* and then worked in the newspaper's engraving department, creating pen-and-ink drawings after photographs of the Boer War

1900
exhibited a drawing at Boston Art Club
moved to New York

1903
married Miriam Rogg

1900–1910
worked as illustrator for *Pearson's Magazine* (New York and London editions), *Frank Leslie's Popular Monthly, Delineator, Designer, Scribner's Monthly, Harper's Bazaar, Century, Everybody's, Cosmopolitan, Success, Life,* and *Women's Home Companion*

1910–1920
lived in Bagnall, Connecticut, renting a house on Den Road
became friends with Gutzon Borglum and painted on Borglum's estate; painted with Frederick Mulhaupt
studied in Cos Cob, Connecticut, with Leonard Ochtman

1912
exhibited for the first time at the National Academy of Design, New York
exhibited at the *First Annual Exhibition of the Greenwich Society of Artists*

1913
became member of the Greenwich Society of Artists; remained a member through 1919

1915
elected academician at the Connecticut Academy of Fine Arts, Hartford

1919
invited by J. Temple Gwathmey, president of the Cotton Exchange, to paint at his estate in Warrenton, Virginia, in the Blue Ridge Mountains; created twenty paintings

1920
returned to New York

1921
produced illustrations of the Crown Point Forts on Lake Champlain for the *New York Tribune*

1923
created images of Fort Ticonderoga for *Harper's Bazaar* and for Stephen Pell, who was restoring the fort; Owen's pen-and-ink sketches were published by Pell in a forty-eight-page book entitled *Sketches of Fort Ticonderoga and Vicinity*

1923–1940
ran his own gallery in New York called R. Emmett Owen: New England Landscapes, located first at 202 Madison Avenue at Thirty-fifth Street. In 1924, the gallery moved to the Rembrandt Building, next to Carnegie Hall on Fifty-seventh Street. By 1935, it relocated to 20 West Fifty-eighth Street, opposite the Plaza Hotel. The gallery's final move was to 681 Madison Avenue, between Sixty-first and Sixty-second streets
spent summers in New England, often in New Hampshire

1931
exhibition of Owen's works held at Greenwich Public Library in Greenwich, Connecticut; show visited by prominent Greenwich residents, many of whom purchased works

1935
exhibition of Owen's paintings at Hood Museum, Dartmouth College

1936
exhibited sixty paintings at Dwight Art Memorial, Mount Holyoke College, Northampton, Massachusetts

1941
moved to New Rochelle, New York, and established a studio there at the Thomas Paine Memorial Museum
exhibitions at the Greenwich Public Library and the New Rochelle Public Library

1950
exhibition, *New England Landscapes by R. Emmett Owen,* held at Albany Institute of History and Art, Albany, New York
solo exhibition of Owen's works held at the Barbizon Plaza Hotel in New York City

1957
died September 14 in New Rochelle, New York

Index to Illustrations